Commission to Assess the Threat from High Altitude Electromagnetic Pulse (EMP): Overview

Threat:
Historical Evidence

- EMP observed during US and Russian atmospheric test programs
- EMP damages and disrupts electronics—does not <u>directly</u> harm people

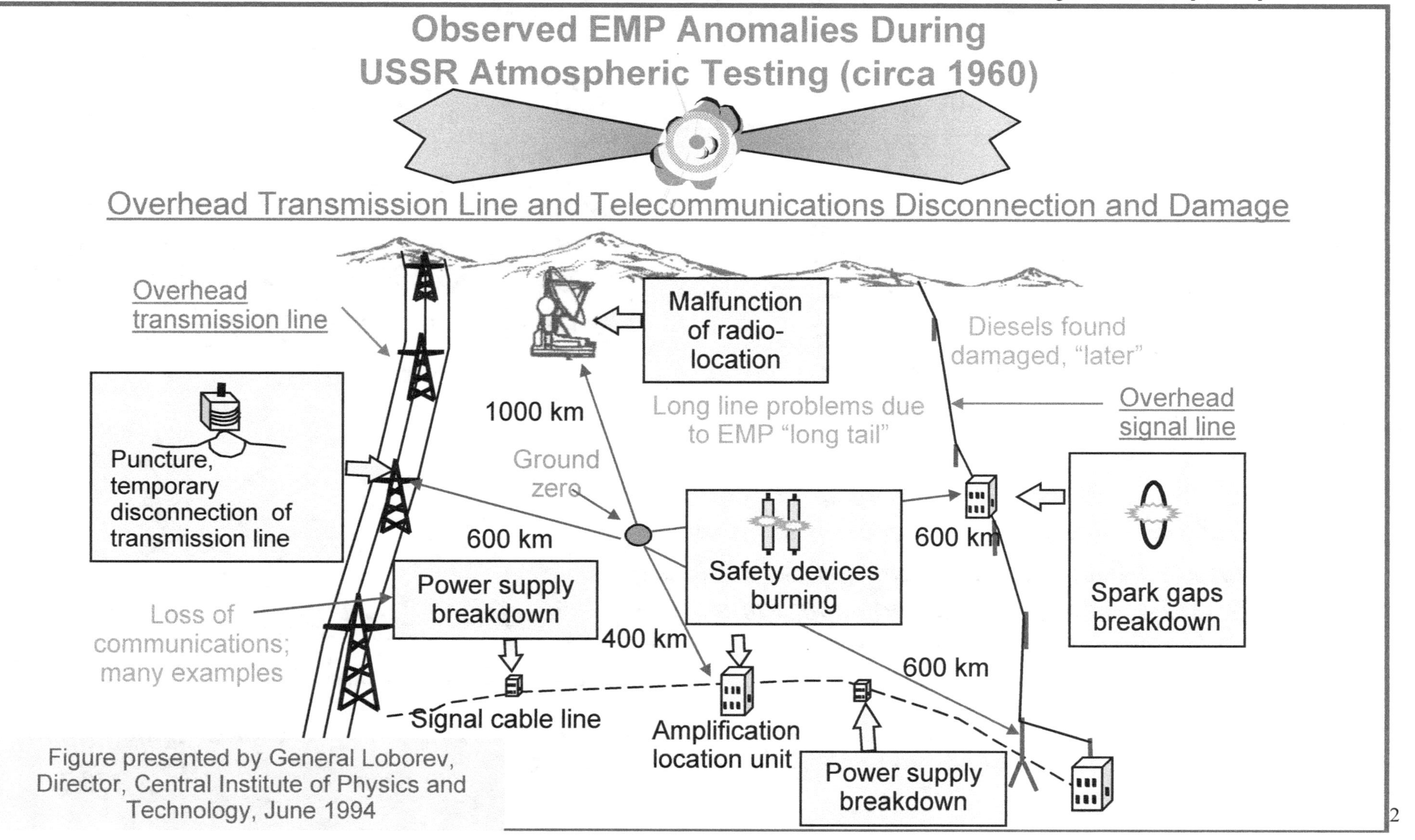

Early-Time HEMP Mechanism (E1)

Weapon-emitted prompt γ-rays

The more individually energetic the γ-rays, the more swiftly they're emitted, and the larger the total quantity of them, the more intense – and the higher frequency – is the HEMP

The induced HEMP pulse and the weapon-emitted γ's both travel at the speed of light, resulting in buildup of large HEMP fields in billionths of a second

B_{Earth}

Compton-scattered air-atom electrons

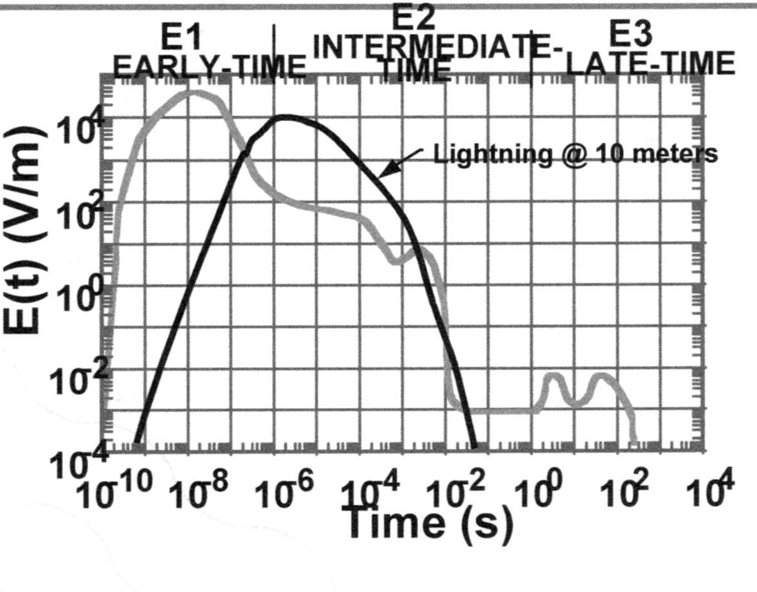

Induced HEMP

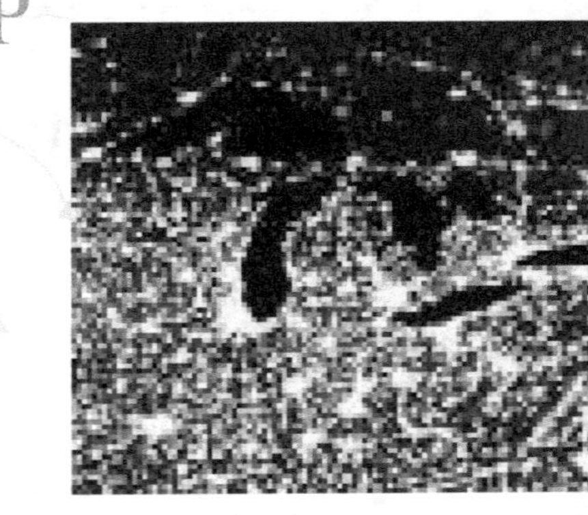

In contrast to the air of near-surface bursts, the thin upper atmosphere allows <u>coherent</u> gyration of the Compton-scattered electrons in the Earth's magnetic field – thus <u>all</u> the g-irradiated atmosphere becomes a titanic antenna

POTENTIAL ADVERSARIES KNOW ABOUT EMP

- "Hypothetically, if Russia really wanted to hurt the United States in retaliation for NATO's bombing of Yugoslavia, Russia could fire an SLBM and detonate a single nuclear warhead at high-altitude over the United States. The resulting EMP would massively disrupt U.S. communications and computer systems, shutting down everything." –Russian Duma Leaders to U.S. Congressional Delegation (May 2, 1999)

- Chinese military writings describe EMP as the key to victory, and describe scenarios where EMP is used against U.S. aircraft carriers in a conflict over Taiwan

- A survey of worldwide military and scientific literature sponsored by the Commission found widespread knowledge about EMP and its potential military utility, including in Taiwan, Israel, Egypt, India, Pakistan, Iran and North Korea.

- Terrorist information warfare [includes] using the technology of directed energy weapons (DEW) or electromagnetic pulse (EMP). (Iranian Journal, March 2001)

POTENTIAL ADVERSARIES KNOW ABOUT EMP-cont

- "If the world's industrial countries fail to devise effective ways to defend Themselves against dangerous electronic assaults, then they will disintegrate within a few years…150,000 computers [belong] to the U.S. Army…if the enemy forces succeeded In infiltrating the information network of the U.S. Army, then the whole organization would collapse…the American soldiers could not find food to eat nor would they be able to fire a single shot."
Electronics To Determine Fate Of Future Wars (Iranian Journal, December 1998)

- "Terrorist information warfare [includes] using the technology of directed energy weapons (DEW) or electromagnetic pulse (EMP)."
(Iranian Journal, March 2001)

- Iran has tested launching a Scud missile from a surface vessel, a launch mode that could support a national or trans-national terrorist EMP attack against the United States.

A WARNING FROM RUSSIAN GENERALS

The Commission met with Russian Generals Vladimir Beolus And Viktor Slipchenko, who stated:

- Russia designed an "enhanced EMP" nuclear weapon

- Russian, Chinese, and Pakistani scientists are working in North Korea, and   could enable that country to develop an EMP weapon in the near future

- North Korea, armed with an EMP weapon, would constitute a grave threat to the world.

States or terrorists may well calculate that using a nuclear weapon for EMP attack offers the greatest utility

- **EMP offers a "bigger bang for the buck" against US military forces in a regional conflict; or a means of damaging the US homeland**

- **EMP may be less provocative of US massive retaliation, compared to a nuclear attack on a US city that inflicts many prompt casualties**

- **Strategically and politically, EMP attack can: threaten entire regional or national infrastructures that are vital to US military strength and societal survival; challenge the integrity of allied regional coalitions; and pose an asymmetrical threat more dangerous to the high-tech West than to rogue states**

- **Technically and operationally, EMP attack can compensate for deficiencies in missile accuracy, fusing, range, reentry vehicle design, target location intelligence, and missile defense penetration**

EMP Commission Charter: Title XIV

Duties of Commission

- **Assess the EMP Threat to the US:**
  - Nature and magnitude of EMP threats within the next 15 years
    - From all potentially hostile states or non-state actors
  - Vulnerability of US military and especially civilian systems
  - Capability of the US to repair and recover from damage to military and civilian systems
  - Feasibility and cost of EMP hardening select military and civilian systems
- **Recommend protection steps the US should take**

Commission considered:
- Only EMP threats produced by high-altitude detonation of a nuclear weapon
- Threat assessment based on present and possible future capabilities of potential adversaries because of 15-year outlook

Commissioners

- Dr. John S. Foster, Jr. (Director LLNL; Director DDR&E)
- Mr. Earl Gjelde (Chief Engineer and Acting Director, Bonneville Power Administration; Under Secretary Dept of Interior, COO, Dept. of Energy)
- Dr. William R. Graham (Chairman) (Director, OSTP; Science Advisor to President Reagan)
- Dr. Robert J. Hermann (Director, NRO; Asst Sec USAF; Vice President, United Technologies)
- Mr. Henry (Hank) M. Kluepfel (VP SAIC; Advisor to the President's NSTAC)
- GEN Richard L. Lawson, USAF (Ret.) (DCINC US European Command; Director Plans and Policy JCS)
- Dr. Gordon K. Soper (PDATSD NCB; Director Nuclear Forces C3; Chief Scientist DCA)
- Dr. Lowell L. Wood, Jr. (Director's Staff LLNL; Technical Advisor, SSCI & HASC)
- Dr. Joan B. Woodard (Exec VP & Deputy Director Sandia National Labs)

Seven Commissioners were appointed by the Secretary of Defense and two by the Director of the Federal Emergency Management Agency

Threat: Nature and Magnitude of EMP Threats
Within the Next 15 Years

- EMP is one of a small number of threats that may

  - Hold at risk the continued existence of today's US civil society

  - Disrupt our military forces and our ability to project military power

- The number of US adversaries capable of EMP attack is greater than during the Cold War

- Potential adversaries are aware of the EMP strategic attack option

- The likelihood of attack depends on the actions we take to be prepared

EMP Coverage for Bursts of Various Heights

- **Wide area coverage**
  - A million square miles
- **Intensity depends on:**
  - Weapon design
  - Height of burst
  - Location of burst
- **Broad frequency range**
- **Threat to all electronics in exposure**

Vulnerability may be an invitation to attack

Vulnerability of US National Infrastructure

- One or a few high-altitude nuclear detonations can produce EMP, simultaneously, over wide geographical areas

- Unprecedented cascading failure of our electronics-dependent infrastructures could result

  - **Power, energy transport, telecom, and financial systems are particularly vulnerable and interdependent**

  - **EMP disruption pf these sectors could cause large scale infrastructure failures for all aspects of the Nation's life**

- Both civilian and military capabilities depend on these infrastructures

- Without adequate protection recovery could be prolonged—months to years

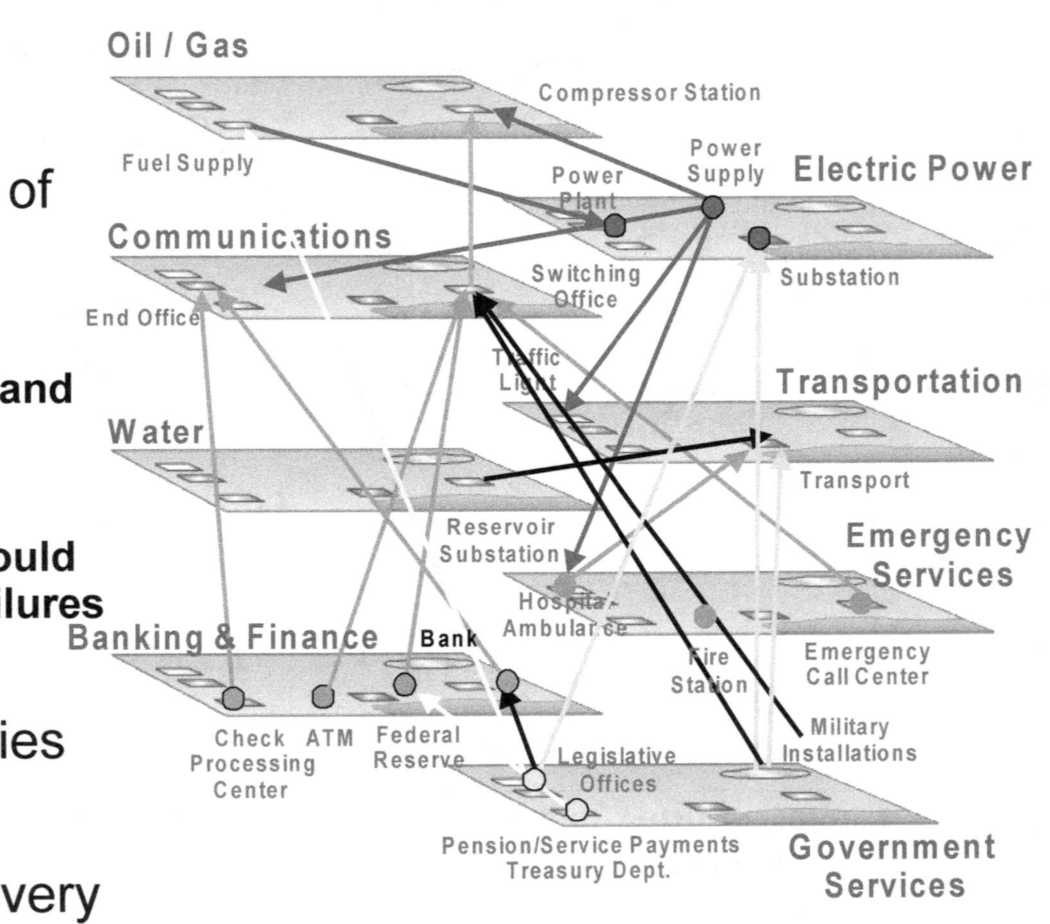

EMP Feasibility and Cost of EMP Protection of Select Civilian and Military Systems

- EMP protection methods are understood and feasible

- Several engineering approaches ensure survivability
  - Shielded enclosures
  - Good grounding techniques
  - Current limiting line filters
  - Terminal protection devices
  - Cable management

- Successful hardening requires testing

- Cost examples for Military Systems:
  - Commission estimates a few percentage points of total system cost
  - For strategic Comm. systems: about 5% or less for life cycle cost
  - To retrofit existing equipment, cost is 15% or even greater

EMP hardening is most cost effective when started in the design phase

EMP Commission Infrastructure Test Activities

- ## Power
  Electromechanical and electronic relays, generator controls, RTU/MTU/DSC/PLC control devices, …

- ## Telecommunications
  wireless cell tower, E911 switch equipment, routers, frame relay switch, modems, corded/cordless phones, IP Data Network elements, NOC equipment,…

- ## Transportation
  cars, trucks, traffic control systems, railroad switches,..

- ## Emergency Services
  police/fire civilian communications devices, mobile command centers, medical equipment/pacemakers, radio/TV,…

- ## Energy Distribution (Gas/Oil)
  SCADA systems, pipeline/pump/valve control systems,…

  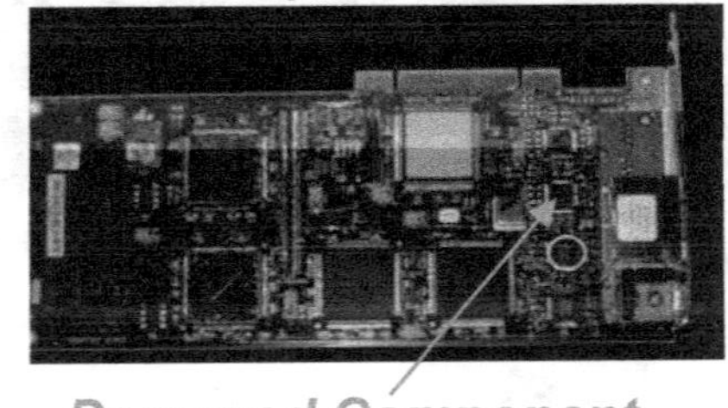
  Damaged Component

- ## Food/Water   *water distribution system controls, refrigerator/freezers…*

- **Supervisory Control Systems (SCADA) are the ubiquitous robots of modern civilization**
  - Process control
  - Environmental monitoring and control
  - Safety of operation
  - Rapid problem diagnosis
  - Real time data acquisition and remote control
- **Generic SCADA may share many component commonalities with PCs**
  - Circuit boards, I/O ports,…

Pipeline SCADA components

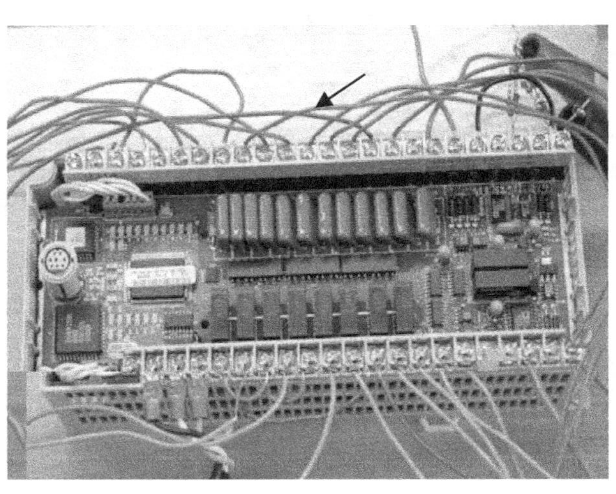

PLC switch activator

Vulnerability of US Electric Power Infrastructure

- EMP induced functional collapse of the electrical power grid risks the continued existence of US civil society
  - Immediate EM transients likely to exceed capabilities of protective safety relays
  - Late time EMP could induce currents that create significant damage throughout the grid
- National electrical grid not designed to withstand near simultaneous functional collapse
- Procedures do not exist to perform "black start"
  - Restart would depend on telecom and energy transport which depend on power
- Restoration of the National power grid could take months to years
  - Typical 500kV transformer is custom tailored to application
  - Spares are seldom available
  - Manufacturing performed offshore
  - Normal delivery time months to more than a year

Substation Transformer

Melted 500kV transformer coil from EM induced flux creating a hot spot

Electric power is key to a functioning society and military. EMP induced destruction of power grid components could substantially delay recovery.

E3: Power Grid Response Modeling

Summary of GIC Flows in US Power Grid for a Multi-megaton Threat

- Collapse of power grid likely for large E3 event

- Large E3 associated with "big" bombs

- Geomagnetic storms provide "natural" simulation of E3 response

— 1989 collapse of Quebec Hydro

-- But, geomagnetic storms may be much smaller than EMP from large nuclear explosions

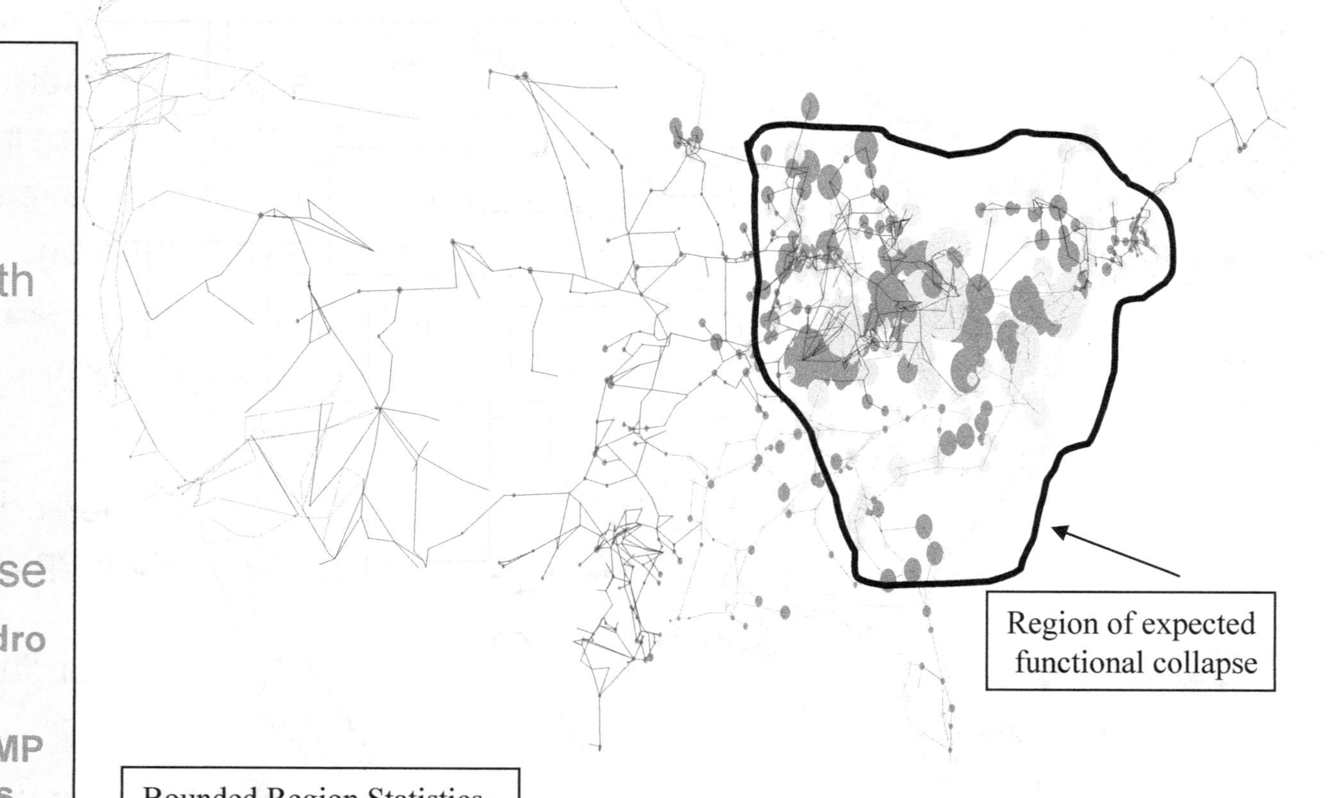

Capability of the US to Repair and Recover from Damage to Civilian Systems

Other Civilian Infrastructures Dependent Upon Availability of Power

- **Telecommunications:**
  - May be significantly impacted, at least at the outset
  - Recovery will be dependent on prompt restoration of power
- **Financial system:**
  - Vulnerable to an EMP induced disruption of telecommunications and computers
- **Remote controls** in infrastructures are at risk of disruption and damage
  - **Transportation** infrastructure is vulnerable to disruption.
  - **Oil and gas supplies** likely disrupted due to failures of pump and valve controls
  - **Potable water** likely disrupted in the region affected by the EMP
  - **Distribution of food** may be degraded
- US scientific and technical capability to address EMP and other nuclear weapon effects has diminished to the point where continued viability is questionable

No credible capability exists to predict the full response of a single system (e.g., national power grid), let alone the highly interdependent US infrastructure

Danger of EMP Attack Can Be Mitigated

- Our free, modern society has inherent vulnerabilities that cannot be completely eliminated

- Catastrophe can be averted by practical and affordable steps to
  - *Prevent* attacks,
  - *Prepare* to recognize and respond to an EMP attack
  - *Protect* critical infrastructure elements and strategic military capabilities, and
  - *Recover* following attack

- National security and homeland security are Federal responsibilities that should be funded by the Federal government

In just a few years we can make significant, affordable improvements to protect society even if an EMP attack is carried out against us

We Can Do Something About it: Strategy and Recommendations

- Pursue Intelligence, Interdiction, and Deterrence to Discourage EMP Attack
  - *highest priority is to prevent attack*
  - *shape global environment to reduce incentives to create EMP weapons*
  - *make it difficult and dangerous to try*

- Protect Critical Components of Key Infrastructures
  - *especially "long lead" replacement components*

- Maintain Ability to Monitor/Evaluate Condition of Critical Infrastructures
  - *absence of information can make things worse either through inaction*
  - *or inappropriate action. Salutary example ~ Blackout of August 13, 2003*

- Recognize EMP Attack and Understand How Effects Differ from Other Disruptions

- Plan to Carry Out Systematic Recovery of Key Infrastructures
  - *demonstrate will and capacity to recover from any attack*

Strategy and Recommendations

- Train, Evaluate, "Red Team", and Periodically Report to Congress

- Define Federal Government's Responsibility/Authority to Act
    - *Governance distributed among Federal, State, regional and variety of non-governmental entities and associations*
    - *DHS has unique responsibility to coordinate homeland response to threat*
    - *DOD has unique responsibility to assure survivability and continued operational effectiveness of our military forces in face of EMP threat*

- Recognize Opportunities for Shared Benefits
    - *planning for rapid recovery/restoration of key infrastructures confers protection against other disruptions; natural, accidental, or advertent*
    - *some protective steps may enhance the reliability and quality of critical infrastructures*

- Conduct Research to Better Understand Infrastructure System Effects and Develop Cost-Effective Solutions to Manage Effects

Strategy and Recommendations

- Homeland Security Council
  - Prioritize government- and society-wide efforts to counter the small number of threats that can hold our society at risk

- Department of Homeland Security
  - Establish a specific, dedicated program for protection of America against society-threatening attacks
  - Establish a senior leadership position with accountability, authority, and appropriate resources for the mission of defending against the most serious threat
    - Develop metrics for assessing improvements in prevention, recovery, and protection
    - Provide regular, periodic reporting on the status of these activities

Conclusions

- The EMP threat is one of a few potentially catastrophic threats to the United States

- By taking action, the EMP threat can be reduced to manageable levels

- US strategy to address the EMP threat should balance prevention, preparation, protection, and recovery

http://empcreport.ida.org